ナンタケットバスケット
ストーリー

── はるか海の彼方から ──

The
Nantucket
Basket
Story

From a Far Away Island

八代江津子

Etsuko Yashiro

撮影：奥谷 仁

Photography : Masashi Okutani

スタジオの一日は朝4時から。暗く静まり返った中、アランの大好きな緑色のカウンターの上で作業が始まる

A typical day at the studio starts at 4 a.m. In the dark calmness, Alan begins work on his favorite green counter.

The Nantucket Basket

ナンタケットバスケットを愛するすべての人へ

For those who love Nantucket Baskets

ゆっくりページをめくるに連れて
バスケットの世界がわかるような絵本を作りたいと思っていました。

最後のページにたどり着く頃には
バスケットとはまるで昔からの友人であったかのように感じられる本になりました。

心ゆくまでこの一冊をお楽しみください。
あなただけのナンタケットバスケットに出会えるまで。

I've been dreaming of writing a picture book that provides a look into the world of
Nantucket Baskets for a while now.

My hope is that you can sit back, relax, and turn the pages at a slow pace.

By the time you get to the last page,
you should feel as if you've known Nantucket Baskets for a long time, just like an old friend.

Enjoy this book to your heart's content,
and may you someday find your own Nantucket Basket.

海にせり出すように立つ家々。海水の温度が上がるのに時間がかかるため、ナンタケットはメインランドより春の訪れが遅く夏は長い

Some houses along the sea. It takes a while for the ocean temperature to rise after the winter. Spring comes late and summer is longer than it is on the mainland.

Contents

ナンタケットバスケットを愛するすべての人へ ………… 3
For those who love Nantucket Baskets

アメリカ東海岸。ボストンの南。ケープコッドから30マイルと少し南の小さな島。 ………… 7
On the East Coast of the United States. South of Boston. A tiny island located 30 miles off the coast of Cape Cod.

捕鯨─島に豊かさを与え、バスケットに命を吹きかける。 ………… 15
Whaling brought richness to the island and gave life to baskets.

「島と捕鯨」 The Island and Whaling ………… 16
「港」 The Port ………… 19
「島」 The Island ………… 20
「想い〜海から」 Thoughts from the Sea ………… 23
「ナンタケット島と日本」 Nantucket Island and Japan ………… 24
「ニューナンタケット」 The New Nantucket ………… 26

─海で生まれ、海で育った、海の似合うかご─ ………… 29
An artisan craft born from the sea, and raised by the sea.

「バスケットの起源」 The Origin of Nantucket Baskets ………… 31
「ライトシップ」 The Lightships ………… 33
「ライトシップの衰退」 Decommissioning of the Lightships ………… 35
「フレンドシップバスケット」 The Friendship Basket ………… 36

バスケット事典 ………… 38
The Nantucket Basket

バスケットの仕組み Anatomy ………… 38
ナンタケットバスケットのパーツ Components ………… 40
ナンタケットスタイル・アクセサリー Nantucket Style Accessories ………… 46
家の中のバスケット Baskets at Home ………… 47

ナンタケットバスケットに関わる職人たち ………… 50
The Artisans of the Nantucket Basket

アラン・リード Alan S.W.Reed ………… 52
八代江津子 Etsuko Yashiro ………… 58
ナップ・プランク Nap Plank ………… 64
ティム・パーソンズ、キャロル・リンクィスト ………… 68
Tim Persons, Karol Lindquist
ビル＆ジュディ・セイル、スーザン＆カール・オッティソン ………… 69
Bill & Judy Sayle, Susan & Karl Ottison
マイケル・ケイン、キャサリン・メイヤー ………… 70
Michael Kane, Kathleen Myers
ジェリー・ブラウン G.L. Brown ………… 71
リー・アン・パペル、マイケル・J・ベニュー ………… 72
Lee Ann Papale, Michael J.Vienneau
ジャック・フリッチ、ジョン・シルビア ………… 73
Jack Fritch, John Silvia

ナンタケットライトシップバスケット美術館 ………… 74
The Nantucket Lightship Basket Museum

楽しい仲間と出会えるナンタケットバスケット教室 ………… 76
Nantucket Basket School

おわりに 感謝の気持ち ………… 78
Gratitude

●ナンタケットバスケットを制作する際に材料となる象牙などについては、それぞれの国の許可のもとに使用、販売しています。

●Basket makers use ivory for carvings to decorate their baskets, which is obtained under strict laws from their respective countries.

Vermont

New Hampshire

Boston

Massachusetts

Rhode Island

Connecticut

Cape Cod

Hyannis

NANTUCKET

ナンタケット島までボストン、ニューヨーク
から飛行機で約40分。プライベートジェッ
トも多いが、最もドラマチックなのはケープ
コッドのハイアニスから1時間の船での入港

Nantucket

It takes 40 minutes by plane to get to Nantucket
from Boston and New York. Many private jets
also fly between these cities, but the most
dramatic way to reach Nantucket is by a one-
hour boat ride from Hyannis in Cape Cod.

New York

New Jersey

Nantucket Island

アメリカ東海岸。
ボストンの南。ケープコッドから30マイルと少し南の小さな島。

On the East Coast of the United States.

South of Boston.

A tiny island located 30 miles off the coast of Cape Cod.

マッコウクジラはこの島のスーパースター。
油は上質で竜涎香(りゅうぜんこう)がまれに
採れるため、船乗りは皆、この鯨を追った

Sperm whales are the superstars of the island.
Because of their fine oil and ambergris, they
were highly sought after by whalers.

18〜19世紀にかけて、ナンタケットは世界の捕鯨の中心でした。
捕鯨技術が確立されたのも、この島。
鯨油をヨーロッパへ輸出し
1840年代には、世界が得る捕鯨の富の3分の2を持つ島とまでいわれ、
今では世界の人々を惹きつける避暑地。
船から見る島はいつも霧に曇り、
その姿からついたニックネームは、
「グレイ・レディ」。

Nantucket was a center for the world whaling industry in the 18th and 19th centuries.
Whaling technologies were perfected on the island.
In the 1840's Nantucket was said to own up to two-thirds of the worldwide profits
gained from whale oil exports to Europe.
Today, Nantucket is a summer resort town attracting people from around the world.
When seen from a boat, the island is almost always cloudy in the mist.
Because of this, Nantucket's nickname is the "Grey Lady".

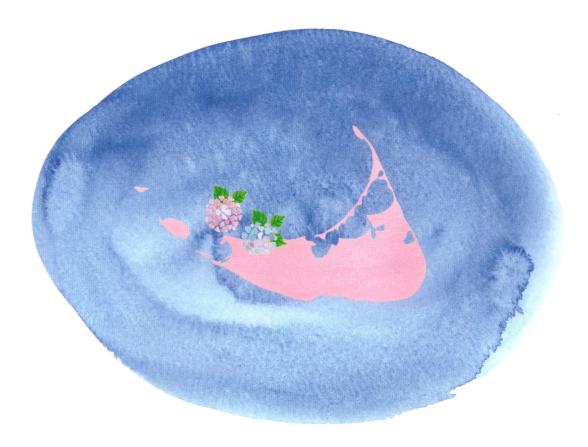

地図でも見落とされるような小さな島が世界のナンタケットと呼ばれるようになり、今では知る人ぞ知る島に

Nantucket is a small island that is easily overlooked on a map. Even still, it is becoming more and more well known around the world.

人口　11,000人（2019年アメリカ合衆国国勢調査）

面積　273㎢

北緯　41度　西経　70度

国定歴史建造物地区（1966年より）

ハーマン・メルビルの小説『白鯨』（1851年）の舞台

　　「この陸地と海とを併せた球体の三分の二はナンタケットびとのものなのだ。

　　然り、海はかれらのものだ。

　　皇帝が帝国を版図とするように海を領しているのだ。」

　　（『白鯨』田中西二郎訳　新潮文庫1952年）

Population: 11,000 (United States Census 2019)

Land Size: 273 km²

Latitude: 41 degrees north

Longitude: 70 degrees west

National Historic Landmark District since 1966

The setting of the novel "Moby-Dick" by Herman Melville

　　"Two thirds of this terraqueous globe are the Nantucketer's. For the sea is his; he owns it,

　　as Emperors own empires;"

　　(Harper & Brothers 1851)

それがこの島、ナンタケット。

This is the island of Nantucket.

基本的な形のシンプルなナンタケットバスケット。バッグとして正式な場所での所持を許されている。八代江津子の作品

A minimal authentic style Nantucket Basket, made by Etsuko Yashiro. This can be used as a purse for formal occasions.

そんな島ではぐくまれたのが、

ナンタケットバスケット。

そのお話です。

In this unique New England island environment,
the Nantucket Basket was born.
This is the story of those baskets.

ナンタケットの街並みを特徴づけているのは、
潮風にさらされて灰色になった杉壁の家々。
この灰色とレンガの赤色が町を彩る

Nantucket is characterized by rows of cedar
houses that have turned gray from exposure to
the sea breeze. These homes, mixed in with the
red bricks, are a hallmark of the town.

Whaling

捕鯨—島に豊かさを与え、バスケットに命を吹きかける。

Whaling brought richness to the island and gave life to baskets.

Small talk of Nantucket

捕鯨船=海賊船!?
大航海時代ならではの知恵

　大航海時代、捕鯨船は海賊船を模した外装をほどこしていました。当時、海賊がしばしば出没し、多くの被害が報告されています。そのピークは1660〜1726年といわれていますが、その後も海賊の襲来は続き、1835年頃まで捕鯨船が航行するカリブ海は海賊フィールドでした。

　The whale boats in the Age of Geographical Discovery were decorated with designs imitating pirate ships.
　Pirate invasions were frequent in those days, and they caused a lot of damage. The peak was said to be between 1660 and 1726, but pirate invasions continued until about 1835. The Caribbean Sea, which whale boats sailed along, was infested with pirates.

「島と捕鯨」

　ナンタケット島は氷河によってつくり上げられた小さな島、ハーマン・メルビルの『白鯨』(1851年)の舞台でもあります。

　島の鯨捕りは、スコンセットと呼ばれる町で始まりました。先住民のワンパノアグ族が、小さなカヌーで沖に出てハープーンと呼ばれる銛で鯨を射止めます。銛で刺された鯨はもがき、海に潜り逃げようとします。この方法で鯨を仕留めるのには多くの危険が伴っていました。しかし、鯨は、大きな栄養源、資源でもありました。浜に揚げた鯨を解体して肉を食用にし、皮下脂肪から油を採取し、骨も利用したのです。

　1641年、島に入植してきたクエーカー教徒たちは、ワンパノアグ族から捕鯨技術を学びます。捕鯨は大きな危険を伴う仕事でしたが、その報酬は大きかったため、彼らは命をかけて捕獲技術をしだいに向上させていきます。

　特にマッコウクジラには多くの魅力がありました。頭部にある脳油は鯨の中でも良質な油で価格も高価でしたし、まれに腸内から竜涎香(香料)を含むこぶし大の結石が採れることからも、捕鯨船のメインターゲットでした。彼らはついに大型船を仕立て、マッコウクジラを追うために大海に乗り出していきます。捕鯨時代の到来です。1691年、ナンタケット島はマサチューセッツ州に属することになり、1700年代から1840年頃まで捕鯨の中心基地として栄えます。1820年にはナンタケット船籍の捕鯨船276隻が世界を回っていました。

　しかし、1855年に油田が開発され、その後廉価な石油が供給されるようになると、燃料としての鯨油の需要が低下していきました。さらに過剰な捕獲がもたらす悪影響などにより、鯨の価値はみるみる下がっていきます。また、港が砂洲で浅かったため、より大きくなった船が出入りできなかったことで、1800年代後半からは捕鯨の基地が本土のニューベッドフォードに変わっていき、さらに1880年には西海岸のサンフランシスコに移っていきます。

　島は衰退を余儀なくされます。1846年に起きた島の大火は、それを決定的なものにしました。捕鯨バブルに沸いた島、ナンタケットは、大きな屋敷と中心基地としてのプライドを残したまま、かつての輝きを失っていきました。

The Island and Whaling

Nantucket is a small island formed by a glacier, and is the setting of Herman Melville's 1851 novel,"Moby-Dick".

Whaling on the island began in a small town called Sconset. In those days, the Wampanoag native Americans went to the sea in small canoes and captured whales with harpoons. It was very dangerous to hunt whales in this way, but the islanders took the risk since whales provided many valuable resources and were a source of nutrition. The islanders pulled the whales they captured to the beach and sliced them into pieces to eat. They extracted oil from the fat, and used their bones. This was the beginning of whaling in Nantucket.

The Quakers, who settled on the island in 1641, followed the Wampanoag and learned whaling. Whaling was very dangerous, but the rewards were so great that they kept hunting whales and risking their lives. Gradually, hunting techniques improved.

Sperm whales in particular were attractive to hunters. The oil in the heads of sperm whales was used as fuel and was sold at a high price. They sometimes found oily balls of ambergris the size of a fist in the gut of sperm whales. This was used to make perfumes. For these reasons, sperm whales were the main target of whaling. Eventually, the whalers built big boats and went out to sea to capture sperm whales. The whaling age had arrived. In 1691, Nantucket became a part of the Commonwealth of Massachusetts and prospered as a central base for whaling from the 1700s to about 1840. As many as 276 registered whaling boats from Nantucket were sailing around the world by 1820.

The demand for whale oil as fuel started to decrease when oil fields were developed and inexpensive petroleum started being used in 1855. Because of this, the price of whales declined sharply. At the same time, whalers were starting to get exhausted from the severe whaling conditions in Nantucket. Additionally, the harbor was shallow, so big boats could not enter. Around late 1800's, the center of whaling moved to New Bedford, Massachusetts, and then to San Francisco, California in 1880.

Nantucket island began to decline. A big fire in 1846 made matters even worse. Nantucket, once a prosperous whaling center, dwindled. There was, however, still a big population of people left on the island who were proud of its history and roots in the whaling industry.

捕鯨全盛期、港には捕鯨船が頻繁に出入りし、鯨油を運ぶ樽で陸は埋め尽くされていた。今はその賑わいはなく、静かな風景が広がる

During the heyday of whaling in Nantucket, many whaling ships were squeezed in and out of this port, and oil barrels filled the land. Today, Nantucket is a much quieter island town.

Small talk of Nantucket

町の石畳にも、捕鯨全盛の頃のなごりが……

　島のメインストリートには、こぶし大の石が敷かれています。歩きにくいことこのうえなく、自転車も自動車も徐行を余儀なくされる石畳ですが、今も大切に保存管理されています。これらの石は捕鯨時代、鯨油を運搬し終えた船に、帰路イギリスでバラスト(重み)として積まれた小石。港に着いて役目を終え、道に敷き詰められたもので、捕鯨時代のなごりとなっています。

　The main streets of Nantucket are covered with fist size cobble stones. It is very hard to walk on these stones, and bicycles and cars are forced to move slowly. The streets, however, are well-maintained even today. The cobble stones came from England during the whaling period. Whale oil was shipped to England, and to weigh down the boat for the return trip, they'd load it with cobble stones. These stones finished their duty upon arriving back to Nantucket and paved the streets. They are a remnant of the whaling era.

「港」

私は、ナンタケット島を初めて訪れる人には、ぜひ船で来てほしいとお伝えしています。島の家々の屋根にはウィドーズウォーク（寡婦の見晴台）という、日本の物干し台に似たバルコニーかベランダのようなものがありますが、洗濯物を干すための場所ではなく、ひさしはついていません。このデッキは航海から戻る家族の船をいち早く見つけるための展望台であり、再び出航する船を最後まで見送る場所だったのです。

捕鯨の全盛期、航海は文字どおり命がけの仕事でした。一度航海に出ると、３か月から３年、いえ二度と戻らないことも少なくありませんでした。

当時は、船長の年齢は若い人では26歳くらい、乗組員の中には11、12歳の少年もいたようです。夫や息子を送り出す女性たちの気持ちは、どれほどのものだったでしょうか。また、二度と会えないかもしれない家族を残して船出する男たちの気持ち、あるいは長い年月を海で過ごして航海から戻るとき、「子供は元気に育っただろうか」「母は変わりないだろうか」「妻は待ってくれているだろうか」など、懐かしさと不安が入り交じる気持ちはどれほどだったでしょうか。そんな当時の人々の心の機微が、この港には詰まっているのです。

だからこそ、初めて訪れる人には、この港から入り、港から出航してほしいと思っています。その当時の景色を想像し、その当時に想いをめぐらせながら。

The Port

I would advise visitors coming to Nantucket Island for the first time to come by boat. Every house on the island has a "Widows' Walk", which is similar to a laundry hanging balcony or veranda in Japan. There are no eaves, as it is not a place to dry laundry. The deck is an observatory to look out on the ocean and see if a family's boat is returning home. It is also a place to watch, as boats sail off and melt into the horizon.

In the glory years of whaling, whalers risked their lives on voyages. It took anywhere from three months to three years for a boat to return from a voyage, and some never returned after setting sail.

In those days, captains were as young as 26 years old. 11 and 12 years old boys were sometimes crew members. I wonder how women felt when sending off their husbands and sons. On the other hand, how would men who chose to be whalers feel once they set off and left their families, possibly to never see them again? Nostalgia and uneasiness among whalers would increase on the way back home after many months and years of sailing. No doubt some wondered, "Has my child been brought up well?" or "Is my mother still alive?" or "Has my wife been faithful?" Such were the subtleties of the heart among people in this jam-packed port.

For these reasons, I want people coming to Nantucket for the first time to sail in and out of the port and imagine the scenery of those days.

「島」

当時の島の女性たちは、鯨捕りに出かけた男たちの留守を守り、家庭や地域を切り盛りしていました。この島では、黒人奴隷はいち早く解放に近いかたちとなり、住人たちと共存していました。それにはクエーカー教徒の勤勉さとリベラルさ、そして、さまざまな人種の乗組員たちが関わっていた捕鯨という産業が影響していたようです。

島の女性は船乗りと結婚し、夫が帰らないのが当たり前。どこかそんな生活を謳歌していた様子がうかがえます。残された女性を中心とした社会で生きることが、ひとつの夢だったようです。

港からメインストリートを上がっていくと、1本目にユニオンストリート、2本目にオレンジストリートと海岸線に平行に走る道があらわれます。その1本目のユニオンストリートは上級船員、2本目のオレンジストリートは、キャプテンたちの住まいが並ぶ道といわれています。そしてメインストリートをのぼりきると、スターバック三兄弟など、船主の豪華な家々が並びます。一般船員は、海辺の「フィッシュ ロット」と呼ばれる地域に住んでいたようです。坂をのぼるにしたがって徐々に家が大きくなっていく様子に、一種の階級というものを感じます。

海から戻る夫や子供をいち早く見つけるため、そして最後まで見送るための場所。「寡婦の見晴台」という名前がもの悲しい

This is a viewing post that allows wives to spot their husbands and children returning from the sea, and to send off their loved ones. They were given the sad name of "Widow's Walk".

The Island

Women on the island in those days managed their houses and their community while the men were away hunting whales. The Quakers on the island were religiously opposed to slavery and had always vouched for abolition, and early whalers were some of the most diverse crews in the ocean—made up of Native Americans, Europeans, freedmen, and even East Asians who came aboard during expeditions.

At the time, many women on the island dreamed about marrying a whaling captain. While many husbands and sons never returned from their journeys, the people of Nantucket still seemed to enjoy this female-centered community.

As you enter the main street of the island from the port, you will come across the first street, called Union Street. After this, Orange Street runs parallel to the sea. Homes for the officers were lined up along Union Street, and those of captains were lined along Orange Street. As you reach the end of the main street, you will find the most majestic homes on Nantucket—those of ship owners like the Starbucks'. On the other end, the lowest paid sailors generally lived in an area called the "Fish Lots", near the beach. Generally, the higher you went up the hill, the bigger the houses got.

Small talk of Nantucket

世界最古のロゴは髑髏マークだった!?

海賊のマーク、髑髏(どくろ)に2本の骨は世界最古のロゴといわれています。シンボルマークとしての意味もさることながら、目的は相手を怖がらせて戦いを最小限に抑えようとした苦肉の策だったようです。それにしてもこの世界最古のロゴ、すばらしい発明です。

The Jolly Roger, a flag with a skeleton and two bones, is said to be the world's oldest pirate logo. The logo symbolizes its meaning clearly —but the logo was actually designed as a deterrent, a last resort to scare people off and minimize battles. Nevertheless, this old logo is a splendid invention.

Small talk of Nantucket

何か月もの捕鯨船暮らし。男たちの仕事場のすさまじさ!

　乗組員たちは船の上で何か月もシャワーを浴びることができませんでした。また鯨が捕れると、船上でも解体作業が行われたため、そのすさまじい悪臭に悩まされていたようです。特にマッコウクジラの頭の中は、辟易する臭いだったといわれています。
　その航海の辛さは、私たちの想像をはるかに超えるものだったのではないでしょうか。

　The crew was unable to shower or bathe while sailing for months at that time. Not only that, every time a whale was captured, it was cut into pieces on board—a very messy process(which involved the smallest crewmember crawling into the whale's skull to "bail out the case").

　The difficulty of life on board is hard to imagine in modern times.

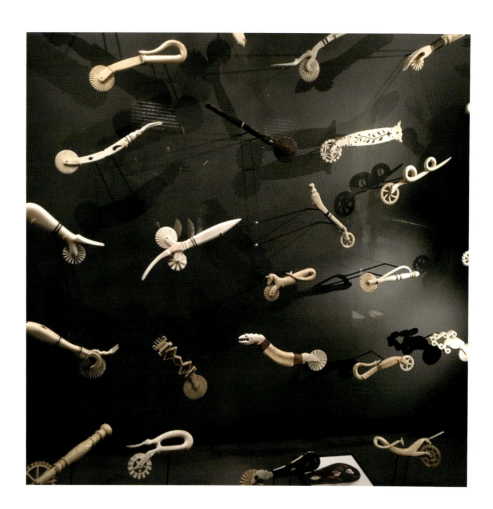

ナンタケット捕鯨博物館に展示されている多くのパイカッター。すばらしいデザインの数々は、もうアートの領域

Whalebone pie cutters on display at the Nantucket Whaling Museum. These intricate carvings are an art piece in itself.

港を出るときにブラントポイント灯台に向けてコインを投げると、またこのナンタケットに戻ってくることができるといわれている

It is said that if you toss a coin into the ocean near the Brant Point lighthouse, you'll be granted good fortune to return to the island.

「想い〜海から」

　大海原への憧れや冒険への期待に胸をときめかせて出航した乗組員たちも、海の上では、何か月もあらわれない鯨や、島への郷愁に胸をこがしていたようです。船上で彼らは、捕獲した鯨の骨や歯でさまざまなものを作りました。
　なかでも、パイカッター(パイを切る道具)が多く作られており、アメリカの文化ともいえる母の手作りアップルパイ、そして母への想いの強さが感じられます。
　また、鯨の歯にスクリムシャウをほどこすこともありました。スクリムシャウとは骨や歯に絵を彫り込んだ工芸品のことをいいますが、クルーたちの必須アイテムであるシーナイフで歯の表面を削って絵を描き、そこに大鍋で鯨の肉を煮たときに出る煤をすり込んで色を入れていたのが、スクリムシャウの始まりです。
　これがアートとして昇華されていきました。

Thoughts from the Sea

The crew, once eager to go out to the vast expanse of ocean and excited for adventure, grew homesick, weary, and frustrated after being on the ship for months without seeing a whale. Crews often crafted using whale bones and teeth to pass the time.

Pie cutters in particular were made frequently, showing how much crews missed their mothers' apple pies, an American tradition. Many mothers were proud of their apple pies.

The crew often scraped the surface of whale bones with boat knives, which were indispensable tools for seamen. They drew pictures and rubbed soot from large pans used for boiling whale meat to create images in the bones—the beginnings of what would become the art of scrimshawing.

ナンタケットの夏は紫陽花に覆われ、一段と華やかな雰囲気に。この島に行くならば夏、7月、8月がおすすめ

Nantucket is covered with hydrangeas in summer, invoking a spectacular atmosphere. July and August are the peak viewing times.

「ナンタケット島と日本」

　ナンタケット島の7月は紫陽花が咲き乱れます。島の中ほどに紫陽花専門の栽培農家があるくらい、島の人々は紫陽花を愛しています。ご存じでしょうか、紫陽花の原産国、故郷は日本です。

　捕鯨が盛んになり、ほぼ世界の鯨が捕り尽くされた頃の江戸時代末期、ナンタケットでは日本近海がマッコウクジラの生息地として知られていました。日本は鎖国により大型船の建造が禁止され、外洋での漁も禁止されていたため、日本近海にはマッコウクジラが多く生息していたのです。

　ナンタケットからの捕鯨船は、たびたび日本近海にもあらわれ、しけに遭うと乗組員たちは日本への上陸を余儀なくされていたようです。鎖国中のため、その報告は幕府にまで届けられることもなく、人道的な理由から多くの日本人が人目をしのんで彼らを助けたようです。

　下田は紫陽花の咲き乱れるところ。ここにも捕鯨船が立ち寄った形跡があります。見たこともないこの美しい花を家族に持ち帰りたい、そんな思いがあったのでしょう。今は、ナンタケット＝紫陽花です(紫陽花についてはシーボルトがヨーロッパに持ち帰り、鯨油の輸出入の際にそこからナンタケットに持ち込まれたのではないか、との説もあります)。

　14歳だった中浜万次郎(ジョン万次郎1827～1898)は土佐清水の漁師でしたが、漁の間にしけに遭い、鳥島まで流されます。そこで捕鯨船に助けられてアメリカに渡り、ナンタケットからほど近いニューベッドフォードで教育を受けました。彼は日本に帰国するまで捕鯨船で航海士として働き、そこで得た資金を元手にカルフォルニアで金の採掘などもしています。

　捕鯨船は、日本近海で捕鯨する際に、水や食料を確保できる寄港地を必要としていました。その要請に応えたのがマシュー・ペリーです。1853年7月8日、ペリーは日本の浦賀に到着します。このことが日本を大きく変えていくきっかけになりました。開国です。

Nantucket Island and Japan

In July, hydrangeas bloom all over Nantucket. These flowers are so beloved by the islanders that some of them became gardeners specializing in hydrangeas.

In the Edo period (1603–1868) in Japan, when whaling was booming and most whales around the world were captured, the sea surrounding Japan was known as a ripe habitat for sperm whales among Nantucket whalers. Japan was still isolated from the world by policy in those days, and Japanese sailors were prohibited from building vessels for long, transoceanic journeys. As a result, the waters around Japan became a favorite spot for sperm whales around the world.

The whalers from Nantucket went around Japan from time to time, and were sometimes forced to make landfall in Japan during severe storms. Such cases were not reported to the Japanese Government, since the policy was to stay secluded. However, even in those difficult and unforgiving times, some Japanese locals went out of their ways to save the lives of shipwrecked Nantucket whalers.

There is a story told of a Nantucket crew visited the Japanese city of Shimoda when hydrangeas were in bloom throughout the city. The crew wanted to take the plant back home. Today, hydrangeas are a symbol of Nantucket. (Some claim that Siebold brought back hydrangeas to Europe, and when they traded whale oil, the flower was brought to Nantucket.)

Manjiro Nakahama (John Manjiro 1827–1898), who was only 14 years old during the Nantucket whaling era, was a fisherman from Tosashimizu who was sailing around Torishima when he encountered a typhoon, which almost drowned him. He was rescued by a Nantucket whaling boat. Once rescued, he asked to be taken back to America so he could explore the world. He was brought back to America and educated in New Bedford, a town close to Nantucket. Manjiro lived an adventurous life, working as a crew member of a whaling boat, and even digging for gold in California.

Whalers needed a port near Japan to supply water and food. It was Matthew Calbraith Perry who responded to the need. Perry landed on Uraga City in Japan on July 8th, 1853. This became the chance to make a big change in Japan—it was time for Japan to open its doors to the world.

マシュー・ペリー、中浜万次郎（ジョン万次郎）の二人は、ともに日米をつなぐキーパーソン。それぞれが捕鯨船との縁も深く……

Matthew Calbraith Perry and Manjiro Nakahama (John Manjiro) were both key players connecting Japan and the U.S. Each had a deep connection with whaling ships.

「ニューナンタケット」

　しばらく忘れられた島だったナンタケットは1950年代、その自然の豊かさ、町の美しさ、家々の大きさから、避暑地としての地位を確立していきます。鯨油の供給基地だったナンタケットの名前は、人々の記憶から完全に消え去ることはなかったのでしょう。

　島は息を吹き返し、ニューヨークなどからセレブリティが自家用機で訪れる避暑地。その中でも代表的な地がスコンセット（Sconset）。通常この短い名称で呼ばれていますが、正式名称はシアスコンセット（Siasconset）です。

　ここは当初、漁師が一時的に滞在する小屋があるだけの村でした。そのために一軒一軒がとても小さく造られ、今でも土間のままの家も少なくありません。ほとんどの家が屋根裏を寝室にして、効率よく造られています。その家々も現在まで大切に保管され、避暑地の住まいとして活用されています。春になると屋根をバラが覆い、紫陽花が家々の周りに咲き乱れます。

捕鯨の始まりは、このスコンセットから。1881〜1917年は町に鉄道が敷かれた。最後の車両は今、レストランに

Whaling started in the town of Sconset. A railway was laid between 1881 and 1917. The last train car is now used as a restaurant.

ナンタケットから世界各地への方向と距離が描かれているコンパスローズ。日本がないのが残念。これはラルフローレンの店の東壁

This compass rose showing directions and distances around the world from Nantucket, on the east wall of the Ralph Lauren store. It's a bit sad that Japan is not depicted.

現存するスコンセット最古の家。居間とキッチンは土間、屋根裏が寝室の小さな家。もともと漁師小屋として1675年に建てられた

The oldest house in Sconset was built as a sea shanty in 1675. It's a small house with a living room and a kitchen on the dirt floor, and a bedroom in the attic.

The New Nantucket

Nantucket, no longer a whaling town, has established its position as the premiere New England summer resort destination thanks to its rich nature, cultural history, and the beauty of its landscapes.

Today, celebrities visit the island in private planes, and the wealthy walk the cobblestone streets. The town that represents Nantucket most is Sconset. The town is usually called by its short name, but its true name is Siasconset.

At first, Sconset was a mere village of fishermen who temporarily stayed in huts during the whaling season, and thus the huts are very small. You will find quite a few houses with dirt floors even today. Most houses use the attic as a bedroom for efficient use of the interior space. These houses are kept meticulously up to date, and are often used as summer houses. In the spring, roses cover the roofs and hydrangeas bloom prolifically around the houses.

Small talk of Nantucket

ナンタケットならでは！
独特の街並みを保つための規制

　ナンタケットでは、14店舗以上を展開している大資本は店舗を出せないというルールがあります。生活に必要なマーケットやガソリンスタンドは規制から外されてはいますが、町の中心地で見ることはありません。ここが、アメリカのどの町とも同じようにならないための配慮だそうです。ナンタケットがナンタケットであるためのルールです。ただし、ラルフローレン社は小さな店舗を構えています。しかし、これも大きく広げることはできません。

　Chain stores with more than 14 shops are prohibited on Nantucket. Supermarkets and gas stations necessary for daily life are exceptions to this rule, but you won't find them in the town center. This rule is designed to help keep Nantucket's unique flavor, and prevent it from becoming like many other cities in America. There is however, a small Ralph Lauren store in the town, but the shop is prohibited from expanding further.

捕鯨船が伝統的なスクリムシャウの手法で描かれている、フラットリッド(平らな蓋)のバスケットパース。アラン・リードの作品

A basket purse made by Alan S.W. Reed, with a flat lid decorated with a traditional scrimshaw etching of a whaling ship.

3点がセットになったネストタイプのオープンバスケット。それぞれに違う種類の鯨の象嵌がほどこされた八代江津子の作品

Three nesting open-style baskets created by Etsuko Yashiro, with three different types of whale inlays.

The Nantucket Basket

—— 海で生まれ、海で育った、海の似合うかご ——

An artisan craft born from the sea, and raised by the sea.

時を経て、ナンタケットバスケットは飴(あめ)色に変色。200年前のバスケットもいまだに魅力を放つ。アンティークバスケット

Over time, the color of Nantucket Baskets turns amber. This antique basket made 200 years ago is still in beautiful shape.

「バスケットの起源」

　ナンタケットバスケットの起源には諸説あります。例えば、先住民ワンパノアグ族が作っていたバスケットから発展したという説。鯨油を入れる樽作りの技術を応用して、船でバスケットが作られたという説。たぶん、そのすべてが絡まりあいながら形成されてきたのだと思います。

　樽職人は捕鯨船に欠かせない存在でした。鯨は捕獲されたあと解体され、材料となる部位は大鍋で加熱されて油となります。その油は樽に保管されます。職人は船に常に乗り込み、樽のメンテナンスも行っていました。その樽を作る技術がナンタケットバスケットの基礎になっていきました。ナンタケットバスケットには底板があります。それはまさに樽の底。材料はオーク。樽にある縦に使われる板はステーブと呼ばれています。バスケットのそれも同じ名称。樽を締めるのは金具の輪、リム。バスケットでは上部の枠をリムと呼びます。

　捕鯨船は鯨を求めて世界をめぐります。大西洋、インド洋、南氷洋、太平洋、そして樽職人はアジアで籘に出会い、バスケット作りを発展させていくのです。マラッカ海峡を渡り切り、寄港地であったフィリピンなど東南アジアで籘に出会ったのではないか、と私は考えています。小さなすべての要素が偶然と必然から出会い、できたのがこのバスケットです。

The Origin of Nantucket Baskcts

　The Nantucket Basket has many roots. Nantucketers were first inspired by woven baskets made by the island's Wampanoag natives, but were further influenced by the oil barrels used by whalers.

　Barrel craftsmen were indispensable on whaling boats. After a whale was captured, the body was cut into pieces and heated in large pans to make oil. The oil was stored in barrels. Barrel craftsmen were always present on boats to maintain the barrels. The design of the Nantucket Baskets resembles that of the oil barrels, and the same materials and techniques are used for both. The same oak base used in the barrels is used as the base of the baskets. The vertically arranged materials in barrels are called "staves", and the same name is used for baskets. A metal fitting, called a rim, is used to hold the barrels tight. The top of many baskets is also called a rim.

　The whalers would travel around the world looking for whales, traversing the Atlantic, Indian, Antarctic, and Pacific oceans, picking up new materials along the way. Once they crossed the Strait of Malacca, they reached the Philippines and Southeast Asia, where they are thought to have discovered rattan—this became a major material in basket making. A number of small coincidences merged to create the materials for the baskets.

Small talk of Nantucket

鯨が余すところなく使われていた時代があった

　アメリカでは鯨の肉は捨てて一部しか活用していないといわれていますが、ワンパノアグ族が鯨肉をジャーキーとして食していたという記録が残っています。当時は、骨はコルセットなどに、髭は釣具などに、現在のプラスチックの代替えとして余すところなく使われていました。

　It is said that the whale meat was usually thrown out, and only a part of it was used in the United States. It is true, however, that there was a time when no part of a whale's body was wasted. Records indicate that whale meat was eaten as jerky by the Wampanoag, and that whale bones were used for corsets prior to the invention of plastics. Whale whiskers were also used for fishing gear.

ナンタケットバスケットは進化してきました。

The Evolution of the Nantucket Basket

年代 Year	作られた場所 Where made	名前 Name	様式 Style	特徴 Characteristics
1700 〜	ナンタケット島 Nantucket Island	ナンタケット バスケット Nantucket Basket *総称としても使われます		ざっくりとした編み目。家の中用。 ステーブには島の木が使われていた。 Simple handiwork. Staves made from local wood. For household use.
1860 〜	ライトシップ Lightship	ライトシップ バスケット Lightship Basket		作り手によりハンドルや ベースの形が異なる。 Artisans experiment with different handle and base shapes.
1950 〜	ナンタケット島 Nantucket Island	フレンドシップ バスケット Friendship Basket		ホセ・レイが考案。 作家がそれぞれの スタイルを確立。蓋付き。 Originated by Jose Reyes. Artisans began to establish their own unique styles with lids.

ボストン港に舫われている現在のライトシップ。4月から10月まで、週末のみ博物館として公開されている

Currently, Nantucket lightships are moored in Boston Harbor. They are open as a museum during weekends in April through October.

「ライトシップ」

　捕鯨船は時とともに大型化し、さらに、より多くの船がナンタケット港に出入りするようになったため、灯台の設置が必要になりました。しかし、港の地形が砂洲のため灯台を建てることが難しく、やむをえず考案されたのがライトシップ。船の上に照明を設置し、沖に停泊させて灯台の役目を担ったのです。
　船はアンカーがおろされていたにもかかわらず、砂洲には固定できず、嵐の夜は一晩で80マイルも沖に流されるということも珍しくなかったようです。一度乗り込めば1～3か月、乗組員は船での生活を余儀なくされました。長い船上生活の間、乗組員たちはバスケットや細工を作り、そのうち島で販売するようになっていきました。彼らはそれぞれの作り方を工夫したため、ひと目で誰の作品かがわかるようにもなりました。お互いの技術を尊重しながら作られたのが、ライトシップバスケットです。その頃、捕鯨が衰退し、捕鯨船の乗組員の多くが灯台船・ライトシップに仕事を求めるようになっていきました。

The Lightships

It became more and more urgent for there to be a lighthouse at the Nantucket port as the boats became larger and more boats went in and out of the island. However, as the topography of the port consisted of a sandbar, it was difficult to build a lighthouse. Inevitably, lightships were built. Lightships were essentially floating lighthouses—lights were placed on the top of offshore ships.

The lightships were anchored to the sandbar, and it wasn't unusual for a lightship to drift as far as 80 miles from the shore on a stormy night. The crew spent about one to three months on board. Having nothing much to do during those periods, crews started making baskets to sell on the island. Crew members got more and more skilled at making baskets, and each basket-maker had their own style. People could tell whose work it was at a glance. The Lightship Baskets were produced in this way and were highly respected for their technique and artistry. The whaling business, on the other hand, started to decline and many crews looked for jobs on lightships.

Sankaty　サンカティ

Brant Point　ブラントポイント

Great Point　グレートポイント

1850年建立。スコンセットの崖に凛(りん)と立ち続けてきた。赤い帯が美しく、まさに灯台といったらこれ、という佇(たたず)まい

Sankaty was built in 1850. It is a lighthouse that stands on the cliff of Sconset. The red broad line of Sankaty beautifully represents an authentic lighthouse.

1746年建立。出入港時に必ず見る背の低い灯台。季節ごとにリースなどが飾られるナンタケット市民のマスコット的存在

Brant Point was built in 1746. It's a short lighthouse that people see when entering or leaving the port. It is decorated with a seasonal wreath, and is adored by the people of Nantucket.

1784年建立。ビーチを40分ほど進んだ先の4輪駆動のみが入場を許される砂地にある。行きづらく、なかなか見ることができない

Great Point was built in 1784. Only four-wheel-drive vehicles are permitted to drive on the sandy beach. It is a difficult 40-minute ride to see the lighthouse.

「ライトシップの衰退」

　ナンタケットに3つの灯台ができたことにより、ライトシップ(灯台船)は必要なくなり、廃止されます。船の中でバスケットを作っていた乗組員たちは陸に上がり、バスケットを作り続けました。

　そんな中、捕鯨船のキャプテンであった祖父を持ち、自らもライトシップのキャプテンを務め、バスケット作家でもあったミッチェル・レイのもとに、一人のフィリピン人、ホセ・レイが訪れます。1945〜1948年頃のことでした。

　ここからバスケット作りが大きな発展をとげていきます。

Decommissioning of the Lightships

After three lighthouses were finally built on the island, the lightships were decommissioned, and the crew members who had been making Lightship Baskets on board brought the craft back to the island with them.

Between 1945 and 1948, a Filipino man named Jose Formoso Reyes moved to Nantucket and met Mitchell Ray, a basket maker and the descendant of a line of whaling boat and lightship captains.

It was at this time an evolution occurred in basket making.

Small talk of Nantucket

マッコウクジラの英語名の由来とは?

　マッコウクジラは英語ではsperm whale。spermは日本語ではヒトの精液です。でもなぜ？ 不思議ですよね。実はマッコウクジラの頭の部分には大きなポケットがあり、そこに良質の油が詰まっています。この油、空気に触れると精液のように白濁するため、そのような呼び名がつけられました。

Sperm whales were given their name because when whalers first cut into the whales' heads, they found a big pocket of a cloudy, thick substance, which, when exposed to air, resembled human sperm. The substance turned out to be a fine, clean-burning oil.

「フレンドシップバスケット」

　ホセ・レイが蓋を制作するまでは、ナンタケットバスケットは蓋のない、シンプルなものでした。ハーバード大学を卒業した彼がナンタケットに住むようになったのは、人種差別などで仕事を得ることができず、妻の故郷であるナンタケットに身を寄せたのが理由でした。ナンタケットでも仕事を得ることが難しく、手持ち無沙汰の日々が続いていたときに、彼は隣人でバスケットの作り手でもあるミッチェル・レイと知り合います。ミッチェルの作るバスケットはホセの故郷フィリピンの籐を使ったバスケットとは少し違うものでした。ホセはミッチェルに師事し、また故郷のバスケットの作り方を伝えました。彼は、もともとモールド(型)を使って作る伝統的な製法を、モールドを使わずに自由に作ってみるなど、試行錯誤を繰り返しました。そして1947年、蓋のあるバスケットを考案します。

　その蓋付きのバスケットは、避暑地となったナンタケットでバッグとして人気を得ていきます。ニューヨークなどから来るセレブリティたちは珍しさも手伝い、こぞってバスケットを購入しました。まるで合言葉のように同じバスケットを持って友達になる、またその珍しさから互いに声を掛け合う、ということからこの蓋付きのバスケットは「フレンドシップバスケット」と呼ばれるようになります。

バスケットはホセ・レイ、飾りはチャーリー・セイルの作品。レザーのストラップと、黒檀(こくたん)の鯨が当時としては斬新

A basket made by Jose Reyes with a decoration by Charlie Sail. The leather strap and whale of ebony were considered novel at the time.

The Friendship Basket

Nantucket Baskets had quite simple shapes until lids were attached by Jose Reyes. Reyes, who graduated from Harvard University, moved to Nantucket, the hometown of his wife, in the late 1940s. Reyes had trouble finding a job in Nantucket. He spent days without work to do until he met his neighbor, Mitchel Ray, who showed him how to make Nantucket Baskets. Ray's baskets were a little different from the rattan baskets made in Jose Reyes' native Philippines. Jose Reyes started teaching Mitchel how he made baskets back home in the Philippines. Reyes began to experiment with different ways of making baskets. Originally, a mold was used to make baskets, but Reyes started experimenting with free form baskets without using molds. In 1947, he began making baskets with lids after continued efforts of making unique baskets.

The baskets with lids became popular as pocketbooks in Nantucket, which by then had become recognized as a summer resort island. Celebrities from New York raced to buy the baskets because they were unique. Carrying the same baskets helped people to become friends and the unique baskets helped people to talk to each other, and thus these baskets with lids began to be called "Friendship Baskets".

時代により少しずつ形が違うバスケット。こんな風にご婦人方が自慢しつつ、おしゃれして持ち歩いていたのかもしれない

Shapes of baskets differ a little according to the times. In decades past, ladies might have carried baskets fashionably with pride.

[バスケット事典]

バスケットの仕組み

Anatomy

バスケットを制作するには材料や部品が必要になります。
作家といわれる人々はこういった部品を自ら作りますが、現在は購入することができます。

You need the following components to make a basket.
Artisans make these components themselves, but you can now buy them.

ノブもしくは
ワッシャー、
ドーム
Knob,
Washer or Dome
(photo: Washer)

トッププレート
Top plate

取っ手
Handle

蓋
Lid

リム
Rim

ステーブ
Stave

ウィーバー
Weaver

ヒンジ（前）
Hinge (front)

ペグ
Peg

ベースプレート
Base plate

ヒンジ（後ろ）
Hinge (back)

トッププレート、取っ手に重ねた素材、ペグ、ワッシャーは鯨の骨材（マッコウクジラの顎部分）製。八代江津子の作品

The top plate, overlay, peg, and washers are made from the jaw of a sperm whale. Basket by Etsuko Yashiro.

取っ手（ダブルハンドル）
Handle (Double Handle)

ノブもしくは
ワッシャー、
ドーム
Knob,
Washer or Dome
(photo:Knob)

カービング
Carving

ペグ
Peg

ラッチ
Latch

ハスプ
Hasp

伝統的で基本的な形のナンタケットバスケット。ラッチ、ハスプ、ペグ、ノブ、上下プレートは象牙製。八代江津子の作品

A traditional and basic style Nantucket Basket. The latch, hasp, peg, knob, top and base plate are all made from ivory. Basket by Etsuko Yashiro.

「バスケットの部品」

バスケットはこのように小さな部品・部位から成り立っています。日常、あまり耳にしたこともないような部品や部位の名前は、捕鯨船内で使われた樽に由来しているものがたくさんあります。

作家たちは、部品、部位をひとつひとつ作り、組み立てていきます。バスケットのタイプにより、使われる部品、部位も違い、またサイズも変わってくるので、その数は膨大です。そのため作り置くことはなく、そのつど必要に応じて作り出すという仕事の流れです。現在は、材料を販売しているところもあり、作る必要がなくなったものも少なくありません。しかし、この部品の作りや、組み立てる工程がバスケットの美しさを作り出すのです。

また部品、部位にはナンタケットバスケット特有のものが多く、バスケットを他に類を見ないものにしています。例えば、ヒンジなどは革にケーンという細くした籐を巻いて作りますが、そのような作りのものはほかでは見られないのではないでしょうか。

Small components

Baskets are made up of many small components. Many of the parts and pieces are named after parts of barrels used for whaling, and thus are not familiar to most people.

Artisans make the components of Nantucket Baskets individually, and then assemble them. The parts and their locations differ widely depending on the type of the basket. Because of the huge variety, artisans do not stock parts or pieces. It is a "made-to-order" production method. Today, there are shops that sell these materials, but the process of making and assembling the parts adds to the beauty of Nantucket Baskets.

Most of the components of Nantucket Baskets are originals, making the baskets quite outstanding. For instance, hinges are made by wrapping a cane (a thinned material of rattan) around a leather strap. You find nothing like that in other baskets.

[バスケット事典]

ナンタケットバスケットのパーツ

Components

どの部品、材料もバスケットの仕上がりに結びつく、とても大切な部分です。
すべての部品、材料を入念に選び、合わせることで、ナンタケットバスケットならではの個性が生まれるのです。

Every single component of the Nantucket Basket is crucial to its final outcome.
The careful selection of every component helps shape the uniqueness
of each Nantucket Basket.

型
The Mold

　ナンタケットバスケットは、型に沿わせながら編む数少ないバスケットのひとつ。モールドと呼ばれるこの型を作るのは、非常に難しいといわれています。モールドにより、作る労力が大きく変わります。

　Nantucket Baskets are one of just a few basket styles that are woven on a mold. The mold determines the shape of the basket, and having a flawlessly shaped mold is very important to the finished basket. Building these molds is also a painstaking process.

トッププレート、ベースプレート
Top Plates and Base Plates

　樽の底板が進化したのがベースプレートとトッププレートです。まったく同じものを使用することもありますが、トップには穴のないもの、ベースにはモールドに固定させるために穴のあるものを使用します。

　これらのプレートはさまざまなサイズの素材で作られます。大きなトッププレートに小さなベースプレート、その逆もあります。それぞれのプレートには溝が彫られ、この溝にステーブを挿して固定し、モールドの型に沿って編むのがこのバスケットの製法です。

　Originally inspired by the flat tops and bottoms of whale oil barrels, or the "heads", the tops and bottoms of Nantucket Baskets are woven around flat, disc-shaped wooden plates. These plates come in many different sizes and materials.

　Each plate is carved with a groove around the edge, where the vertical staves are inserted. Once inserted, the basket maker weaves cane (a thinned material of rattan) through these staves, staying tight against the mold to mimic its shape.

ステーブ（バスケットの縦の部分）
The Staves (vertical part of a basket)

バスケットの縦軸となるステーブには、島に古くから自生していたオークを伝統的に使用してきました。通常、木工には木材を半年から2、3年乾燥させて使いますが、ステーブとして使う場合は、木材が乾燥する前に細く切り出し、冷蔵庫などで保存して使用します。一度も乾燥させたことがないという点が重要ですが、切り出すことが難しく、職人にとってはいちばんの腕の見せどころです。

現在はオークのほかに、、チェリー、メープル、ウォールナットなどが使用されています。また、鯨の髭を使うこともあり、非常に扱いづらいのですがフレキシブルで強い素材です。籐を入手できるようになってからは、籐はウィーバーのみならずステーブとしても使用されています。柔らかいので扱いやすく、耐久性もあります。

バスケットの作り手にとって、重要で難しい工程のひとつが、モールドの丸みに沿ってステーブの先端を切っていくテーパーという技術です。ステーブは下から上まで同じ隙間に仕上げる必要があるので、正確にテーパーすることが要求されます。ステーブが乾燥して硬くなる前にこの作業を終えなければならず、複雑な型のバスケットほど技術が要求されるのです。

The vertical "staves" on a Nantucket Basket are traditionally made of raw oak, as it was historically plentiful on the island. Fresh, undried wood must be used, to preserve the flexibility and fine edges.

Oak is still the most popular, but it is not uncommon these days to find staves made of cherry, maple, walnut, or even whale baleen—though this last is a very difficult material to work with. Since rattan has become more readily available, it has also started to be used as staves, rather than just for weavers.

One important and particularly difficult step for the basket maker is to taper the stave ends to match the curve of the mold. Since the staves of the finished basket must have the same gap from the bottom to the top, the tapering must be exact. Not only that, all of this tapering must be done before the wood has a chance to dry, becoming brittle and unforgiving. Oddly shaped baskets need even more technique to master.

ウィーバー（縦のステーブを編んでいく素材）
Weaver (a material to weave the vertical stave)

ナンタケットバスケットの初期の作り手は、柔らかめの木材や樹皮を使用していましたが、捕鯨船が東南アジアの港に立ち寄ったときに籐に出会い、ウィーバーとして使用されはじめました。籐を細くしたウィーバーをケーンといい、バスケットの大きさにより太さを決めます。インドネシア、フィリピン、中国などが原産で、ナンタケットバスケットには最高品質の籐だけが使われます。

どのような形のバスケットも編み目が波打たないように注意して編み進めますが、複雑な形の場合はウィーバーが上下するためにステーブがデコボコとなりやすく、高い技術が必要となります。

Nantucket's first basket makers started by using soft wood and bark. However, once the whalers began sailing to Southeast Asia, they discovered rattan—a strong, flexible reed-like material that was perfect for weaving baskets. Rattan is thinned to cane for use as a weaver. A subtropical plant, rattan is imported from Indonesia, the Philippines, and China. Only the highest quality rattan can be used for Nantucket Baskets.

Regardless of the shape of the basket, the cane must be carefully woven through the staves as to not create any gaps and bumps while ensuring the staves stay perfectly vertical. It takes many years for a basket maker to master this technique.

ナンタケットバスケットのパーツ
Components

取っ手
Handles

　バスケットには持ち運びが楽なように木製の取っ手がつけられていますが、これがないものもあります。最近では、持ちやすいように革製の取っ手なども使用されています。ホセ・レイが考案した革を三つ編みにしたストラップは伝統となっています。また木製の取っ手に象牙などを這わせる、オーバーレイ（取っ手を２種類の素材で作る手法）も最近は取り入れられています。

　The basket usually has a wooden handle for easy portability, though there are also handle-less designs. More recently, leather handles have become popular, making them easier to hold. The braided leather straps designed by Jose Reyes have become a classic design. Another recent decorative touch is the overlay handle, where a layer of ivory is attached to a wooden handle.

リム
Rims

　リムとは、バスケットの上部にある枠のことです。伝統的なものは木で作られます。木を煮たり蒸したりして曲げていきますが、木の素材によっては裂けたり折れたりするので、細さと曲げる角度は非常に気を使うところです。また、継ぎ目を目立たせないためには技術が必要とされます。素材はオーク、チェリー、メープル、ウォールナット、リード（籐の内側部分素材）などが使用されています。

　The rim is the frame at the top of the basket. Traditionally, they are made of wood, bent by boiling and steaming—its thickness and the angle of bending must be carefully considered, as it will tear and break depending on the type of wood. In addition, a special technique is required to hide the seams in the wood. Rims are commonly made of oak, cherry, maple, walnut, reed (the inner part of rattan), etc.

ヒンジ
Hinges

　バスケットの蓋と本体をつなぐ要のパーツです。革の紐に細くした籐（ケーン）を巻きつけて作ります。リムの厚みを考慮して長さを決めていく、高度な技術を必要とする部品です。
　ラッチやハスプをヒンジで作ることもあります。

　The hinge connects the lid to the basket. It is made by wrapping a cane around a leather strap. Making a proper hinge requires considerable skill.

　In some cases, latches and hasps are also made with hinges.

ノブ、ワッシャー、ドーム
Knobs, Washers and Domes

　ノブは、バスケットでは2種類の部材の名称として使われています。
　メインで使うのは、取っ手用の部品として（1.2）。
　取っ手は釘でバスケット本体に取りつけますが、木製部分と金属（釘の頭）が直接当たらないようにするのがノブの役割です。シンプルな突起型、貝や花がモチーフのノブなどがあり、代用として、丸い円盤のようなワッシャーやドームを使うこともあります。素材は牛の骨、象牙、そして木、アクリルなど。
　もうひとつのノブの意味は、蓋用のつまみ（3.4）。木製の蓋をつける場合のつまみとして使うのがノブです。木製や白い素材を使った装飾品がよく使われます。

　In Nantucket Basket making, the "knob" means two things.

　The most common meaning is the knob that connects the handle to the basket（1,2）. This is so the metal nail does not directly contact the wooden rim. In addition to simpler washers and domes, there are several designs for knobs such as shells and flowers. Knobs, domes, or washers can be made of cow bone, ivory, wood, and acrylic.

　The other meaning of "knob" is a button-shaped handle for a carved wooden basket lid（3,4）. These lid knobs can be made of wood or a more decorative material.

43

ナンタケットバスケットのパーツ
Nantucket Baskets Components

ハスプ、ラッチ、ペグ
Hasps, Latches and Pegs

バスケットを開け閉めをするためのパーツです。正面につけますが、バスケット本体につけるものをハスプ、蓋部分に装着するものをラッチといいます。ともに通常は象牙、牛の骨などの堅牢な素材で作られますが、最近は木で作ることもあります。こちらは壊れやすいので使用に注意が必要です。

そのラッチとハスプをつなぎ留めるのが、ペグという小さな鉛筆状のものです。こちらも同素材で作ります。

ペグの大きさとラッチの穴とハスプの突起部分を隙間なく作るのが非常に難しく、またラッチの可動部分の制作には熟練が必要とされます。

Latches, hasps, and pegs lock the basket lid closed. They are attached to the front of the basket; the one attached to the basket is called the "hasp", while the one attached to the lid is called the "latch". Both are usually made of hard and solid material such as ivory and cow bone, but some recent designs have used wood. Carving hasps is an extremely delicate and difficult process.

A small pencil-like part called the "peg" is used to lock the latch and hasp together. This is usually made of the same material.

When making them, it is difficult to make the hole of a latch and the projection of a hasp without gaps, and thus, skill is required to make the moving part of the latch.

スカート
Skirt

アラン・リードが考案したもので、バスケットのリムの下に取りつける木製、または象牙製の装飾です。衣服のスカートのようなので、こう呼ばれています。スカートの模様にはいろいろなパターンがあり、バスケットに優美な表情をプラスしてくれます。

The basket skirt, invented by Alan S.W. Reed, is a wooden or ivory decoration that is attached to the bottom of the basket rim, and resembles a skirt. It adds a gentle touch to the basket, with a variety of different patterns.

ブラスハンドルネイル、ブラスピン
Brass Nails and Pins

　ナンタケットバスケットには、伝統的に真鍮（ブラス）製の釘が使われます。やはり、船上で生まれたかごだからでしょうか。真鍮は潮にあたっても腐食しにくいといわれ、よく船などに使用されています。

　取っ手を取りつける釘をブラスハンドルネイル。そしてリムなどを本体に取りつける小さな釘をブラスピンと呼びます。

　真鍮製の釘は、通常の鉄の釘よりかなり高価なものです。

The nails and pins used for the Nantucket Basket is traditionally brass, perhaps because the basket was first made on boats. Brass was said to be resistant to sea corrosion.

The nails to attach handles are the handle nails made of brass. The small nails to attach the rims on the basket are called brass pins.

These days, brass hardware is much more expensive than a regular iron nail.

カービング
Carving

　小さな彫刻（カービング）で作られる装飾品のこと。ナンタケットバスケットの蓋の上に好みで飾られます。

　カービングはバスケット作家ではなく、カービング作家が作るのが常で、通常、象牙や鯨の歯の素材を好きな形に彫刻してもらいます。鯨の形がナンタケットではよく使われますが、花やカモメなども好まれるモチーフです。

In Nantucket Baskets, the carving is a small decorative sculpture, traditionally made of ivory, bone, or whale tooth. A favorite carving is adorned on the lid of the Nantucket Baskets.

Carving is usually not done by basket artisans, but by carving specialists and scrimshanders. The shape of a whale is a lasting favorite on Nantucket, though flowers, shells, and seagulls are also frequently seen.

ナンタケットスタイル・アクセサリー

Nantucket Style Accessories

ここ10年、ナンタケットバスケットの製法を生かしたアクセサリーが人気を博しています。
若い世代の心をつかむ伝統からのアレンジ。
新しい形や意匠が次々と出ているのが楽しい分野です。

Over the last decade, Nantucket Basket style accessories have become more popular.
This tradition is capturing the interest of many younger people.
It is a fun field in which new styles and designs are always emerging.

1.ミニチュアバスケットのペンダントトップ。小さな中にも大きなバスケットと変わらない技術。贅沢に胸元につけたい。ナップ・プランクの作品。2.フラットなバスケットの上部に見立てたミニチュアがペンダントトップに。エレガントな形の中心に貝やヒトデなどさまざまな飾りをつけて楽しむ。3.バングルは男女問わず身につけられることもあり、人気が高い。太さもいろいろ選べるので、いくつも欲しくなる。八代江津子作

1.Tiny, intricately crafted miniature basket pendant top. A luxurious work by Nap Plank. 2.Miniature flat lid design, used as a pendant top. Various decorations such as shellfish and starfish forms its elegant center. 3.Nantucket bangles are popular among both men and women. Various widths are available. Etsuko Yashiro's work.

家の中のバスケット

Baskets at Home

ナンタケットバスケットはさまざまなライフスタイルを持つ人々に愛されています。
家の中でのバスケットは決して存在を主張しすぎることなく、
さりげなく品よく収まります。

Nantucket Baskets are loved by people in various walks of life.
These baskets are often placed decoratively in houses.
There they can exist elegantly and nonchalantly.

1.家の中にいくつあっても邪魔にならないバスケット。日常使いに取り入れて。一箇所に集めると、すっきりとしたコーナー演出が可能。2.このトレイには、ベースプレートに貝のカービングが。そのままインテリアとして置いておきたい。3.ワインクーラーとして、あるいは花を飾ったりするときにも使える筒型のバスケットも作られている。4.大きなバスケットは何を入れてもきれいに収まるので、おしゃれな収納ツールとして大活躍

1.Baskets do not get in the way, no matter how many there are in the house. In fact, they can be of daily use. When gathered in one place, they will produce a neat accent corner. 2.This tray has shell carving on its base plate. 3.Some artisans make wine coolers, which can also be used as flower vases. 4.Large baskets can serve as a very useful and stylish storage containers.

Nantucket Island

ナンタケット島はグレイ・レディとも呼ばれています。
上品なブルーグレイで彩られる、宝石のような島。
キーワードは、捕鯨、海、紫陽花。そして、バスケット。

Nantucket Island is also called the "Grey Lady".
The island is a historical, picturesque gem, tinted in sophisticated blue-grays.
Drenched in the tradition of whaling, the sea, blooming hydrangeas, and Nantucket Baskets.

The Artisans
ナンタケットバスケットに関わる職人たち
The Artisans of the Nantucket Basket

「作家」

バスケットをひと目見ると誰が作ったか判断できるのが、このバスケットの特徴でもあると思います。それほどに、それぞれの作家が創意工夫を凝らし、独自の世界を広げているのです。

1994年、私はナンタケットを初めて訪れ、その島のバスケットに魅了されました。そして、島の作家であるアラン・リードのバスケットに恋をして、彼に師事することを決心します。

もちろん、簡単には受け入れてもらえませんでした。

それから5年間懇願し続け、ついに弟子となり、バスケット技術を学びました。ずっと島の外に出さなかった技術を文化の異なる他国の私が得るのは簡単ではありませんでしたが、5年の月日をかけてアラン・リードとの信頼関係を作り上げることは、今思うと必要な月日でした。その間に島との縁は深まっていきました。いろいろな人との縁ができていきました。

私の愛するナンタケットバスケットに関わる、島の友人たちを紹介します。

アーモンドと呼ばれる自作のモールド（バスケットの型）を使ったアラン・リードの気品ある作品。フルラッチタイプの留め具は象牙

A basket by Alan S.W. Reed, made from an "almond" shaped mold of his design, paired with an ivory full latch set.

Nantucket Basket Makers

A trained eye can tell who made an artisan-level Nantucket Basket at a glance. Each craftsman puts his/her ingenuity into their work, establishing a unique style.

In 1994, I visited Nantucket for the first time, and was fascinated by the baskets of the island. I fell in love with the baskets made by a renowned artisan Alan S.W. Reed, and became determined to master the craft under his guidance.

Of course, it wasn't that easy. Alan refused to take me as an apprentice. Who was this foreign woman, wanting to learn a craft closely guarded on the island for hundreds of years?

I continued begging him for five long years, making trips to Nantucket just to go to his workshops. Finally, he gave in. Despite our language barrier and my inexperience at the time, Alan taught me everything he knew about Nantucket Baskets. Over those five years he refused to teach me, I deepened my connection to the Nantucket community, hopefully earning some of their trust.

Here are some of my dear friends on the island involved in Nantucket Baskets.

Alan S. W. Reed
アラン・リード

バスケット作家
Nantucket Basket Maker

細かく整然とした目のバスケットを作り、
アランはアラン、といわしめる独自の世界観を持った作家。
ナンタケットバスケットを芸術の域に昇華させました。
材料作りにこだわりを持ち、その技術の高さ、美しさには定評があります。
長年住んだナンタケットから2016年にケープコッドに移住。
2019年にバスケット作家として第一線から退きました。

An artisan who makes detailed and orderly baskets.
Reed has helped elevate Nantucket Basket making into the realm of art.
He has created his own view of the art.
He has a reputation for his high skills and the beauty of his baskets.
In 2016, he moved from Nantucket to Cape Cod.
Alan S.W. Reed has been in partial retirement as a basket maker since 2019.

リー・アン・パペル作のスクリムシャウがほどこされた象牙のスカートとトッププレート。フルラッチはタツノオトシゴがモチーフ

An ivory skirt and a top plate with plenty of scrimshaw, and a seahorse-shaped full latch set. Scrimshaw by Nantucketer Lee Ann Papale.

スカートにさまざまな貝のカービングをあしらったオープンバスケット。色合いのコントラストや形がなんとも上品で清楚

An open basket with various shell carvings on its skirt. The nuance of colors and shapes is so elegant and sophisticated.

ナンタケットバスケットをはじめ、アラン・リード個人のコレクションが飾られた棚。多くはないが、すばらしい作品ばかり

Some of the baskets from Alan S.W. Reed's personal collection. While small, the collection includes some of the greatest works of Nantucket basketry.

ダブルハンドル、貝が飾られたスカート、フルラッチ、そして幸運を呼ぶというカブトガニのカービング。すべて象牙

A carving of a horseshoe crab, a sea creature that supposedly brings good luck. Full latch set, paired with a double handle and basket skirt decorated with shell. All ivory.

日本向けに作られた作品。マンモスの牙で作られたフルラッチやシンプルなトッププレートの飽きのこないデザイン

An Alan S.W. Reed basket made specifically for Japanese collectors. Timeless and simple mammoth ivory full latch set, with a minimalist top plate.

Alan S.W. Reed

In the Studio
スタジオにて

アラン・リード、ナップ・プランク、八代江津子。
三人が思い思いにバスケットを創作し、制作するスタジオ。
時間を忘れ、ひとつの空間を共有するなんとも不思議な場所。

With Alan S.W. Reed, Nap Plank and Etsuko Yashiro.
Where these craftspeople create their intricate works of art.
A creative space where time stands still.

ケープコッドにあるアランの大きなスタジオ。たくさんの道具や機械が所狭しと置かれている。すべて、ナンタケットバスケットを部品からていねいに作るために欠かせない

Alan's large workshop in Cape Cod, filled end-to-end with tools and machines—everything necessary to make his masterpieces and the components of baskets himself.

スタジオの香りはバスケットの香り。その中で、ナンタケットバスケットの伝統、技術、未来に関する話に熱中して一日が終わっていくこともしばしばだった

The workshop is filled with the smells of basket making. Among these aromas, we spend all day talking about the tradition, techniques, and future of making Nantucket Baskets.

張り詰めた空気とあたたかさのミックスした、懐かしいナンタケットの工房にて。いろいろな部品が天井からぶら下がっている雑然とした様子が心地よく、うれしい

Mixed with the warm and tense air of basket making, materials hang from the rafters, at the nostalgic Nantucket studio. Sometimes, I find the clutter and noise to be comforting.

57

Etsuko Yashiro
八代江津子（著者）

バスケット作家
Nantucket Basket Maker

1996年からバスケット制作を始める。アラン・リード 唯一の弟子。
伝統的なバスケットを好み、基本を常に大切にしている。
作家活動だけではなく、ニューイングランドナンタケットバスケット協会、
日本ナンタケットバスケット協会を立ち上げ、
日本、世界へナンタケットバスケットを普及する活動を行っている。

Etsuko Yashiro started making Nantucket Baskets in 1996.
She is the only apprentice of Alan S.W. Reed.
She prefers traditional baskets and believes in always improving the basics,
as well as practicing new techniques.
In addition to her activities as an artisan,
she launched the New England Nantucket Basket Association
and the Japan Nantucket Basket Association,
and is always working to promote the art of Nantucket Baskets to Japan
and the rest of the world.

1999年の作品。ダブルハンドル。さまざまな素材で作った貝のカービングコレクションをふんだんに載せたお気に入りの作品

A piece from 1999, with a distinctive double handle design. A personal favorite, adorned with plenty of shell carvings, each made from a different material.

トッププレートの象嵌部分も含め、ウォールナット材で仕上げたラウンドバスケット。小ぶりでも深さがあるので使いやすい

A round basket, finished with walnut, including the inlaid parts. Small but easy to use because of its depth.

前をシンプルなボタンにして仕上げた作品。革のヒンジとの組み合わせがおもしろい。おとなしい印象ながら洗練されたデザイン

A clever and sophisticated modern design with a simple button clasp, made with a modified leather hinge strap.

59

著名なジュエリー作家、マシュー・フェルドマンとコラボしたパーティ用クラッチ。タイトルは「伝統とコンテンポラリーの出会い」

"Contemporary Meets Tradition", a collaborative piece created with jeweler Matthew Feldman. The piece is a clamshell shaped party clutch.

チャーリー・セイルの珍しい3Dセミクジラを飾った、楕円の典型的ナンタケットバスケット。象牙をふんだんに使った贅沢なデザイ

A typical oval-shaped Nantucket Basket adorned with an unusual three-dimensional right whale carving, made by Charlie Sail. A luxurious design using plenty of ivory.

Etsuko Yashiro

パーティ用にというコンセプトで、小ぶりの
新しい形を制作。すっきりと持てるバッグ。
ふたつの蓋をヒンジでつないで作っている

A new clamshell clutch created from two
hinged lids, designed specifically for attending
parties. This bag is small and easy to carry.

日本の茶道の野点籠(のだてかご)として制作
した横長バスケット。フルラッチ、飾りの貝
やカブトガニのカービングは鯨の骨で制作

This decorative full latch basket, adorned with
whalebone carvings, was designed to hold a
Japanese tea ceremony set.

すっきりとしたデザインに仕上げたマンモスの牙のフルラッチ。小ぶりなバスケットとラッチの大きさのバランスが絶妙

A mammoth ivory full latch set finished with sharp clean lines. Balancing the size of the basket with the latch can be tricky.

横長のバスケット。直線的なラインの黒檀の蓋は、取っ手に沿って上にスライドして開くスタイル。洗練されたモダンなテイスト

A horizontal basket. The straight-line ebony lid slides up along the handle and opens. It exhibits a sophisticated modern taste.

photo:Toshiki Yashiro

Etsuko Yashiro

紫檀（したん）のスカートとマンモスの牙のフルラッチ。トッププレートはメープルのコブ部分を使用。シックな雰囲気ながら華がある

A refined but decorative piece with a rosewood skirt and mammoth ivory latch set. The top plate is made of knotted maple.

Nap Plank
ナップ・プランク

バスケット作家
Nantucket Basket Maker

アラン・リードと長年、工房をともにした作家。
繊細なミニバスケット作りを得意としています。
その作品の可憐(かれん)なテイストには定評があり、
ラッチ作りなどの細かい作業にも才能を発揮しています。

An artisan who has worked with Alan S. W. Reed for many years.
Nap's specialty is in making delicate mini-baskets.
Noted for his intricate designs and meticulous attention to detail.

ハート型のショルダーバッグ。ペグに的矢の形をあしらうのがナップのユーモア。ストラップは革を三つ編みにしたもの

In typical romantic fashion, Nap pairs a heart-shaped shoulder bag with an arrow-shaped peg. Finished with a brown braided leather strap.

取っ手、フルラッチ、トッププレート、カービングすべてに黒檀を使用した作品。取っ手とレザーストラップの両方がついている

Another heart-themed piece, finished with ebony for an unexpected contrast. This remarkable piece has both a handle and strap.

入れ子タイプのオープンバスケット。8個が同じ高さに重なるフォルムがみごとな美しさ！直径15mm〜95mm

Nesting set of eight open baskets, whose rims line up perfectly when placed one within the other. (Diameter: 15 mm-95 mm)

1800年代に作られた蓋付きの小物入れを模したミニバスケット。小さいほど精巧な技術が必要。直径42mm

A miniature, in the style of a 19th century basket. This finely detailed piece requires intericate skill. (Diameter: 42mm)

Nap Plank

きっちりと蓋の閉まるタイプの小物入れ。大きなハートのカービングにナップ・プランクらしさが表現されている。直径60mm

An accessory basket with a tightly fitting wood-rimmed lid and a characteristic Nap Plank heart carving. (Diameter: 60mm)

ミニサイズのピクニックバスケット。蓋とダブルハンドルの素材は象牙。アクセサリー入れに。直径70mm

An adorable mini picnic basket with a tiny working hinged antique ivory top and double handle. (Diameter: 70 mm)

67

Tim Parsons
ティム・パーソンズ

バスケット作家
Nantucket Basket Maker

さまざまな素材を使う作家です。
大ぶりのバスケットはもちろんのこと、
バングルなどのアクセサリーにナンタケットバスケット技術を応用し、
工夫を凝らした創作活動をしています。

Tim Parsons uses various materials.
He stays creative by making not only large baskets,
but also accessories such as bangles
using his Nantucket Basket techniques.

Karol Lindquist
キャロル・リンクィスト

バスケット作家
Nantucket Basket Maker

画家の夫と工房を共有し、
小さなバスケットから大きなゆりかごまで
細部にこだわりながらバスケット作りをしています。
あたたかく気さくな人柄が作品にあらわれている作家です。

Karol Lindquist shares a workshop
with her husband, a painter,
and makes detailed baskets of all sizes,
ranging from hand-held purses to full-sized cradles.
Her warm and open personality can be seen in her works.

photo:Robert Frazier

Bill & Judy Sayle
ビル&ジュディ・セイル
バスケット作家
Nantucket Basket Maker

夫婦でシンプルなバスケットを作り続けています。
黒檀やアンティークの象牙を使った
フラットなトッププレートが特徴のバスケットが代表作です。
スカート付きのバスケットも作っています。

A husband-and-wife team that continues to collaborate
in making intricate baskets in tasteful style.
Their signature style uses flat, unadorned top plate,
with finishes in antique ivory or ebony.

Susan & Karl Ottison
スーザン&カール・オッティソン
バスケット作家
Nantucket Basket Maker

この二人も、夫婦でバスケットを作り続けています。
素朴な中にも、洗練されたテイストを感じさせる
バスケット作りを得意としています。
リー・アン・パペル(スクリムシャウ作家)はスーザンの姪にあたります。

Another husband-and-wife team, Karl and Susan.
They make rustic baskets with sophisticated air.
A family tradition,
Susan's niece is scrimshander Lee Ann Papelle.

Michael Kane
マイケル・ケイン

バスケット作家
Nantucket Basket Maker

タイトなバスケットを作る実力派として有名です。
宝石をあしらうなど、新しい手法にも果敢に挑戦しています。
2019年春、2020年の引退を宣言しましたが、
息子が代を継いでいくべく修業中です。

Michael Kane is famous for making tightly knit baskets.
He boldly challenges incorporating gemstones in his work.
In 2019, he declared his intent to retire in 2020.
Fortunately, he is training his son to take on the family tradition.

Kathleen Myers
キャサリン・メイヤー

バスケット作家
Nantucket Basket Maker

みごとに調和した、芸術的なバスケットを手がける作家です。
写真のような、高さをそろえた入れ子式のオープンバスケットなど、
精密さを要求される構造のものを
ていねいに作る巧みな技術を持っています。

Kathleen Myers makes neat, perfectly tuned works of art.
As seen below, she specializes in nested open baskets of uniform height.
She is a careful artisan with the advanced skills
required to make highly technical basket designs.

G.L.Brown

ジェリー・ブラウン

バスケット作家
Nantucket Basket Maker

3代にわたるバスケット作家の家系。
蓋部分も木のステーブで作るなど、
しっかりとした力強い印象のバスケットを作る技術を
代々大切に受け継いでいます。

G. L. Brown is a third-generation basket maker,
who makes his own lids out of wooden staves.
This skill, which gives a solid and firm impression to his baskets,
has been carefully passed down from generation to generation.

Small talk of Nantucket

かつてナンタケットにあった おしゃれな店で買った宝物

2000年あたりまで「ウィーズ」というおしゃれなセレクトショップがありました。ジョージ・デイビスというデザイナーが経営する店です。彼がウエッジウッドのナンタケットシリーズをデザインしました。自宅用にとウエッジウッドに注文したナンタケット柄の食器がウエッジウッドに気に入られて、製品化されたのです。

私は彼の最後の版画を、彼から直接購入しました。バスケットと有名ブランドのバッグ、その当時あったマーケットの紙袋が書かれた、ちょっとした風刺画です。また、彼がデザインしたナンタケットバスケット型の缶は、閉店と同時に地元のチョコレートショップに引き渡され、しばらくはチョコレート入りで販売されていました。

その缶も版画も、私の宝物です。

バスケットをモチーフにした品々。缶、リトグラフともにウエッジウッドのナンタケットシリーズをデザインしたジョージ・デイビスの作品

Some items with basket motifs. George Davis designed cans and lithographs for the Wedgwood Nantucket series.

Until around 2000, there was a stylish interior shop called Weeds, run by a designer named George Davis. The Nantucket-Basket-inspired patterns he ordered from Wedgwood for private tableware ended up becoming so beloved that Wedgwood incorporated it into its own line of plateware.

I purchased this last print art directly from him. It's a little caricature of seagulls in their nests, the Nantucket Basket, a grocery paper bag and a designer label bag. He also designed small round tins printed with a Nantucket Basket design, which he gave to a local chocolatier when Weeds eventually closed. The chocolatier sold them as little chocolate-filled gift tins.

These basket tins and print are now part of my treasured collection.

Lee Ann Papale
リー・アン・パペル

スクリムシャウ作家
Scrimshander

島を花でかたどるデザインを考案した作家。
島に残る二人のスクリムシャウ作家の一人で、
ナンシー・チェイス(2016年没、最後のカービング作家)は叔母です。
アラン・リードとのコラボレーションが多い。

Lee Ann Papale is a scrimshander who specializes in floral Nantucket designs.
She is one of the only two scrimshanders left on the island.
Nancy Chase, the last carving artisan who died in 2016, was Lee Ann's aunt.
Lee Ann has collaborated many times with Alan S. W. Reed.

Michael J. Vienneau
マイケル・J・ベニュー

スクリムシャウ作家
Scrimshander

島に残るもう一人のスクリムシャウ作家。
主に鯨の歯、骨などに伝統的な工法で描写します。
得意とするリアリティあふれる鯨のカービングは、
しばしばバスケットの蓋を飾ります。

Michael Vienneau is a traditional scrimshaw artist
who primarily carves designs into whale teeth and bones.
He is the other scrimshander currently living on the island.
His realistic whale carvings decorate the lids of many Nantucket Baskets.

Jack Fritsch
ジャック・フリッチ

アンティークバスケット研究家
Historical Researcher of Antique Baskets

ナンタケット島にアンティークショップを持ち、
アンティークのバスケットを扱っています。
ナンタケットバスケット、そしてナンタケットの歴史の研究家で、
日本の食文化にも精通しています。

The owner of "Antique Depot" in Nantucket,
Jack Fritsch is an expert who buys and sells antique baskets.
He continues his research on Nantucket Baskets and its history,
and also has a passion for Japanese food culture.

John Silvia
ジョン・シルビア

アンティークバスケット研究家
Historical Researcher of Antique Baskets

島で唯一のナンタケットバスケット専門店、「シルビア」オーナー。
ナンタケットバスケットはオートクチュールが多く、
作家に直接オーダーし、完成を待つことがほとんどですが、
この専門店では、商品をすぐに購入することが可能です。

The owner of the only Nantucket Basket specialty shop on the island, "Silvia".
A finely crafted Nantucket Basket is considered haute couture,
and people commission custom pieces from specific artists.
But at this shop you can purchase ready-made ones.

The Nantucket Lightship Basket Museum

ナンタケットライトシップバスケット美術館

The Nantucket Lightship Basket Museum

ナンタケットの町の中心から少し外れた場所に、この美術館は立っています。
ケープコッドスタイルハウスを改造してできた小さな美術館は、
絵本に出てくるような愛らしさで人々を迎えてくれます。

This museum stands a little off the center of the town of Nantucket.
The small museum, which was renovated from a small Cape Cod style house,
welcomes people with its picture book-like loveliness.

この美術館には代々伝わるバスケットだけでなく、新しいスタイルのバスケットも収蔵されており、毎年5〜10月までの開館中、年ごとの新しいテーマに沿ってバスケットが展示されます。伝統を守りつつ新しいチャレンジを忘れない美術館です。小さいながらギフトショップにはバスケットにちなんだ商品が並び、若者を育成するためのクラスも開催されているのです。

このように美術館は、さまざまなイベントを通してバスケットの伝統を伝えていく役割を担っています。ナンタケットバスケットを愛し、その伝統をつなぎ続けていこうと、運営は寄付とボランティアで行われています。年に一度、寄付を募るパーティ「ナンタケットバブリー」が海辺のヨットクラブで開催され、バスケットを持ったご婦人たちで賑わい、華やかで夢のような場面が繰り広げられます。

Here, you'll see generational baskets and also newer style baskets. The museum, open from May to October holds exhibitions on a theme set each year. It is a museum that challenges new styles while keeping old traditions alive. Though small, the gift shop is filled with products related to baskets. They also hold classes for youth to foster the values of basket making.

The museum plays a vital role in conveying basket traditions through events and exhibits, and is managed by donations and volunteers who feel a passion for the art of the Nantucket Basket, and are determined see the tradition thrive. Every year, the Nantucket society people, baskets slung in hand, gather along a seaside yacht harbor for The Nantucket Bubbly, a yearly fundraising party to collect people and raise donations from the museum's patrons.

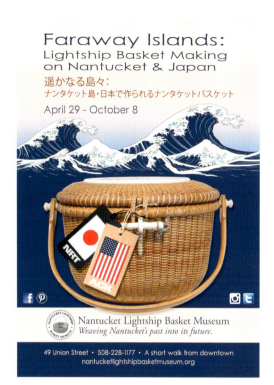

ナンタケットならではの様式を持つこの小さな家が、ナンタケットライトシップバスケット美術館。周りを取り巻く庭の花々も美しい

The Nantucket Lightship Basket Museum is in this quintessential Nantucket style house, surrounded by garden flowers.

ナンタケットのあちこちに、こんな表示が。島の人の愛情がいたるところに感じられ、バスケットが大切にされているのがわかる

Images of baskets are exhibited through out the town to reflect the affection that people on this island have for this homegrown tradition.

毎年違うテーマが設定され、個人所有のバスケットなど、見たことのないバスケットに出会える機会になっている

Every year, a different theme is set for the exhibition, and baskets from around the world are loaned to the collection.

2018年に企画された展示テーマは"ひき継がれるもの"。 私と母の作品が、並べて展示され、思い出深い

The theme for the 2018 exhibition was "What have I inherited?" My mother's works and my works were displayed side-by-side.

2016年の展示テーマは"遥かなる島々：ナンタケット島・日本で作られるナンタケットバスケット" 日本で作られた作品が認められた記念すべき年

The theme for the 2016 exhibition was "Faraway Islands: Lightship Basket Making on Nantucket and Japan". It was a commemorative year when baskets made in Japan were first recognized at the museum.

75

Nantucket Basket School

楽しい仲間と出会える
ナンタケットバスケット教室

ナンタケット島から預かった技術を世界の人に伝えていきたいと
1999年、「ニューイングランド・ナンタケットバスケット協会」を立ち上げました。
島の人々や協会のメンバー、スタッフに支えられ、20年が経ちました。
これからもナンタケットのこの技術を世界に広めていきたいと思っています。

To convey the skills that I acquired from Nantucket Island to the world,
I launched the New England Nantucket Association in 1999.
Since then, twenty years have passed, supported by the island's people,
members of the association and staff.
It is my intention to expand the values of Nantucket Basket making to the world.

Nantucket Basket Association

ニューイングランドナンタケット協会（1999年設立）
日本ナンタケットバスケット協会（2016年設立）
現在（2019年）、日本の協会認定の講師は97名、協会の会員数は2000名を超えていますが、
まだまだナンタケットバスケットの認知度は高くありません。
協会では日本での認知度を上げ、また講師の教育に重きをおき、その技術を後世に伝えていく活動をしています。

New England Nantucket Basket Association (established in 1999)
Japan Nantucket Basket Association (established in 2016).
Today in 2019, there are about 97 accredited lecturers in Japan, and more than 2,000 association members.
Our association attempts to raise awareness of Nantucket Baskets in Japan, and to train qualified lecturers to pass on
their skills and knowledge to future generations.

島を訪れ、専門家から直接バスケットの歴史
や技法を学ぶ。スクリムシャウ作家のリー・
アン・パペルを囲んで

Learning the history of baskets from expert
lecturers, and skills directly from Nantucket
Basket artisans like scrimshander Lee Ann
Papale (pictured,center).

「日本のナンタケットバスケット」

　日本で最初にナンタケットバスケットが紹介されたのは、40年ほど前のデパートでの販売と聞いています。そのときのナンタケットバスケットは、中国で生産されたものでレプリカでした。

　それからしばらくは、日本ではそのレプリカが本来のナンタケットバスケットとされてきましたが、30年ほど前、ブティックなどでナンタケットの職人が制作したバスケットが販売されるようになり、ファッション界に一石を投じます。

　そして1997年、私がナンタケットバスケット制作技術を得たことから日本で教室を開講、現在では日本全国で教室が開催されています。

　2016年にはナンタケットライトシップバスケット美術館にて、「遥かなる島々：ナンタケット島・日本で作られるナンタケットバスケット」というテーマで日本とナンタケット、アメリカの交流を密にしていく展示会も開かれました。

　日本でナンタケットバスケットの人気が高まってきたことから、日本とアメリカの親善の役目も担っています。

Nantucket Baskets in Japan

　The first Nantucket Baskets in Japan appeared at a department store about 40 years ago. These were replicas of Nantucket Baskets, produced in China.

　For a while, in Japan those replicas were regarded as original Nantucket Baskets. It was only about thirty years ago, when baskets made by Nantucket artisans started to be sold at boutiques, it stirred up a controversy in the fashion world.

　In 1997, the time when I acquired enough skills to make Nantucket Baskets, I opened a classroom in Japan. Today, many lecturers and I teach classes all over Japan.

　In 2016, at the Nantucket Lightship Basket Museum, an exhibition themed "Faraway Islands: Lightship Basket Making on Nantucket & Japan" was held. This exhibition highlighted the growing connection between Japan, Nantucket, and the United States.

　As the popularity of Nantucket Baskets has increased in Japan, these baskets help to strengthen the bond between the two nations.

多くのパーツが美しいバスケットになるのを待っている。下の写真は、ケンブリッジ、グレイミスト（著者、八代江津子の店）

Basket parts and tools, ready to be used on a new Nantucket Basket (lower picture: the author's basket shop, GrayMist, in Cambridge).

おわりに 感謝の気持ち

Gratitude

バスケットを作りはじめると時を忘れます。
常に自分との闘いでもあるバスケット作りは
私の拠りどころでもあり、癒やしでもあります。
そんなバスケットに関われる仕事に就けたことは、私の一生の宝物です。
その宝物を少しでも皆さんとわかち合いたい、
皆さんの宝物探しをお手伝いしたい、
そんな想いで歩いてきた25年でした。

アメリカ生まれのバスケットを通して世界を見ることは
アメリカと日本、そして世界を考える機会ともなりました。
また、バスケットを通して多くの人に出会い、
一生の仲間を得ることもできました。
このバスケットは人生そのものでした。

この本を出版するにあたり、声をかけてくださった写真家の奥谷 仁さん、
そして1冊目の本からお付き合いいただいている編集者、北浦佳代子さん、
この本の出版を決めてくださったK&M企画室の関 薫さんには
心からの感謝を申し上げます。

最初から翻訳にあたってくださった小早川裕子さん、
翻訳校正のティモシ・ニューフィールズさん、
全体の校閲・校正でお世話になった山﨑淳子さん、
忍耐強くお付き合いいただき、本当にありがとうございました。

デザイナーの渡邊貴志さん、イラストレーターの竹脇麻衣さんにも
大変感謝いたします。
そして最後まで英訳を手伝ってくれた八代祥季、ありがとう。

また、私のアメリカ人化した日本語を直してくれた
ボストンの友人、松本ヤスコ、ロビン・五味、
そして私を支えてくれているグレイミストスタッフ、ありがとう。

いろいろな情報を提供してくださった
ナンタケットライトシップバスケット美術館の元館長メリーアン・ワシック、
現館長のアンドレア・ウォルフレフ、
理事のスイーティーこと、デリル・ウエストブルック、ペギー・カフマン、
本当にありがとうございます。

走り回る私を見守り、身体のことをいつも心配してくれる家族、
ケニー、利季、祥季、ジュリア、そして母と亡き父、弟。
感謝してもしきれません。口に出してなかなか言えないけれど。

アラン、ジェーン、私を受け入れてくれてありがとう。感謝しています。

最後に、協会のインストラクター、そして生徒の方々にお礼を。
皆さんが私に愛情と信頼を寄せてくださったからこそ、今があります。

心より皆さんに感謝いたします。
ありがとうございました。

2019年秋　八代江津子

――― ナンタケットバスケットを愛するすべての人へ

When I start to make baskets, I forget about time. Making baskets, which has always been a challenge for me, has also always been a source of personal healing. Creating the perfect basket is my lifetime aspiration and a treasure I would like to share with the world. In that way, I want to help you find your treasures. Twenty-five years have passed with such thoughts, as I work in my studio.

To see the world through this truly American art form has given me the opportunity to think about America, Japan and the world. I was also able to meet many people from all over the world and from all walks of life, through my work with Nantucket Baskets, and I've gained lifetime companions along the way.

On the occasion of publishing this book, I would like to express my sincere thanks to Masashi Okutani, who is a photographer and has constantly encouraged me; Kayoko Kitaura, editor for the first edition of my book; and Kaoru Seki from K&M Kikakushitsu, who made the decision to publish this book. Thank you.

I would also like to thank my translators, Yuko Kobayakawa and Shoki Yashiro, and my proofreaders, Timothy Newfields and Atsuko Yamazaki.
Thank you for all your patience.

And thank you Takashi Watanabe and Mai Takewaki for your beautiful design and illustrations.

I also would like to extend my gratitude to my friends, Yasuko Matsumoto and Robin Gomi, and the GrayMist staff, who always watched over me and without whom none of this would have been possible.

Thank you also to Maryann Wasik, a former director of the Nantucket Lightship Basket Museum; Andrea Wallef, the present director; Deril Westbrook, known as "sweetie" of the board; and Peggy Kaufman, for providing various information.

It is hard to say face-to-face, but I cannot say thank you enough to my family, who watches over me running around and always worries about me. Kenny, Toshiki, Shoki, Julia, my mother and late father, and my younger brother—thank you.

Alan and Jane, thank you for accepting me. I am forever grateful to you.

Lastly, I would like to say thank you to the instructors and students of the association. I am what I am today because of the love and trust you have extended to me.

Thank you, all of you, from the bottom of my heart.

Etsuko Yashiro
Autumn, 2019

——— To all people who love Nantucket Baskets

ナンタケットバスケットは唯一公式のパーティで持つこと、そしてテーブルの上に置くことが許されている

Only Nantucket Baskets are considered as official party baskets and are allowed to be placed on the table as a special exception.

主な参考文献
"A Walk Down Main Street -THE HOUSES AND THEIR HISTORIES"
Nantucket Preservation Trust (2006)
"AWAY OFF SHORE -NANTUCKET ISLAND AND ITS PEOPLE", 1602-1890: Nathaniel
Philbrick : Penguin Books (1994)
"Early Nantucket - AND ITS Whale Houses" : Henry Chandlee Forma
Hastings House (1966)
"Images of America-NANTUCKET" : James Everett Grieder and Georgen Charnes :
Arcadia Publishing (2012)
"Main Street, 'Sconset -THE HOUSE AND THEIR HISTORIES" :
Nantucket Preservation Trust (2012)
"Nantucket -A History for Kids" : Patricia Pullman : Gray Lady Books (1988)
"THE DECORATIVE ARTS AND CRAFTS OF NANTUCKET" : Charles H. Carpenter Jr,
and Mary Grace Carpenter : DODD,MEAD (1987)
"Vintage Nantucket" : A.B.C. Whipple : DODD,MEAD (1978)
"Wreck of the Whale ship Essex -The extraordinary and Distressing Memoir that
Inspired-Herman Melvill's Moby-Dick" : Owen Chase : ZENTH PRESS (2015)

「天理大学アメリカス学会ニューズレター」No.48
「文学の中のアメリカ生活誌」(39)
新井正一郎(天理大学国際文化学部教授)、天理大学アメリカス学会(2003)

The Nantucket Basket Story
ナンタケットバスケット
ストーリー

2019年10月25日　第1刷発行
2019年12月10日　第2刷発行

著　者　八代江津子(やしろえつこ)
発行者　関　薫
発行所　株式会社K＆M企画室
　　　　〒102-0074　東京都千代田区九段南1-5-6　りそな九段ビル5F
　　　　https://www.k-and-m.com

印刷・製本　株式会社美松堂

定価はカバーに表示してあります。

造本には十分注意しておりますが、乱丁・落丁(本のページ順序の間違いや抜け落ち)の場合はお取り替えいたします。
購入した書店名を明記して株式会社K＆M企画室あてにお送りください。
ただし、古書店で購入したものについては、お取り替えできません。
本書の一部あるいは全部を無断で複写・複製することは、法律で認められた場合を除き、著作権の侵害となります。
また、業者など、読者本人以外による本書のデジタル化は、いかなる場合でも一切認められませんのでご注意ください。

©Etsuko Yashiro 2019 Printed in Japan
ISBN978-4-909950-01-7 C0076

八代江津子
Etsuko Yashiro

PROFILE

1994年、初めて訪れたナンタケット島でバスケットに出会う。1996年、パット・ケーン氏からバスケットの基礎を習得する。その後、ナンタケット島のバスケット制作の第一人者、アラン・リード氏に師事し、現在に至る。1999年に正式にバスケット制作教育を目的とした「ニューイングランド・ナンタケットバスケット協会」を設立、ケンブリッジ市、ブルックライン市、サンフランシスコ市、サンノゼ市、ロサンゼルス市にてクラスを開催。2005年よりナンタケットライトシップバスケット美術館に作品が展示され、ナンタケット島にてナンタケットバスケット制作者として認知される。2006年、「グレイミスト・エンタープライズ」を設立、ナンタケットバスケット材料店、グレイミストショップをボストン近郊ケンブリッジ市、東京・南青山に展開。2016年、「日本ナンタケットバスケット協会」を設立、日本にナンタケットバスケットを紹介している。現在、マサチューセッツ州ボストン近郊のコンコード市内に夫と住んでいる。

https://nantucketbasket-nenba.com

In 1994, Etsuko Yashiro first encountered baskets on Nantucket Island, and in 1996, first studied under Pat Kane to learn the basics of basket making. After that, Yashiro studied under Alan S.W. Reed, a renowned basket maker on the island . Formally established the "New England Nantucket Basket Association" to promote basket making training in 1999, with classes in Cambridge, Brookline, San Francisco, San Jose, and Los Angeles. Yashiro's works have been continuously exhibited at the Nantucket Lightship Basket Museum since 2005, and she has become recognized as an accomplished basket maker. In 2006, she established "GrayMist Enterprise Inc.", with basket material shops and gifts stores in Cambridge, and Minami-Aoyama, Tokyo. In 2016, the "Japan Nantucket Basket Association" was launched, with the goal of introducing Nantucket Baskets to wider populations in Japan. Today, Etsuko Yashiro lives with her husband outside of Boston, in historic Concord, Massachusetts.

翻訳　小早川裕子（東洋大学国際教育センター准教授）
撮影　奥谷 仁　八代江津子
デザイン　渡邊貴志（ワタナベデザイン）
イラスト　竹脇麻衣
校正（日本語）　山崎淳子
校正（英語）　Timothy Newfields（東洋大学経済学部教授）
編集協力　北浦佳代子
英文協力　Shoki Yashiro　Julia Basil